CASE CLOSED

VOLUME 4

Gosho Aoyama

Case Briefing:

Subject: **Jimmy Kudo a.k.a. Conan Edogawa**
Occupation: **High School Student/Detective**
Special Skills: **Analytical thinking and deductive reasoning, Soccer**
Equipment: **Bow Tie Voice Transmitter, Super Sneakers, Homing Glasses, Stretchy Suspenders**

The subject is hot on the trail of a pair of suspicious men in black when he is attacked from behind and is administered a strange substance which physically transforms him into a first grader. When the subject confides in the eccentric inventor Dr. Agasa, they decide to keep the subject's true identity a secret for the safety of everyone around him. Assuming the new identity of first-grader Conan Edogawa, the subject continues to assist the police force on their most baffling cases. The only problem is that most crime-solving professionals don't want to listen to a little kid. And to make matters worse, the subject's close friend Rachel is beginning to suspect that little Conan and Jimmy may actually be one and the same person.

Table of Contents

CASE CLOSED Vol. 4

Gollancz Manga Edition

STORY AND ART BY
GOSHO AOYAMA

English Adaptation
Naoko Amemiya

Translation
Joe Yamazaki

Touch-Up & Lettering
Walden Wong

Cover & Graphics Design
Veronica Casson

Editor
Andy Nakatani

UK Cover Adaptation
Sue Michniewicz

© 1994 Gosho AOYAMA/Shogakukan Inc.
First published by Shogakukan Inc. in Japan as "Meitantei Conan."
English publication rights in United Kingdom arranged by Shogakukan Inc.
through VIZ Media, LLC. U.S.A. and Tuttle-Mori Agency. Inc., Japan and Ed Victor Ltd., U.K.
New and adapted artwork and text © 2005 VIZ Media, LLC.
This edition published in Great Britain in 2005 by Gollancz Manga,
an imprint of the Orion Publishing Group, Orion House, 5 Upper St Martin's Lane,
London WC2H 9EA, and a licensee of VIZ Media, LLC.

1 3 5 7 9 10 8 6 4 2

The right of Gosho Aoyama to be identified as the author of this work has been asserted by
him in accordance with the Copyright, Designs and Patents Act 1988.

A CIP catalogue record for this book is available from the British Library

ISBN 0 575 07752 2

Printed and bound at
Mackays of Chatham, PLC

www.orionbooks.co.uk

BEIKA MUSEUM...

Medieval Art Exhibit ......

FILE 1: THE ARMORED KNIGHT

HMPH! YOU WON'T LAST LONG AS A SECURITY GUARD WITH THAT ATTITUDE!!

WISH I HADN'T GOT STUCK DOING THE NIGHT SHIFT HERE AT THE MUSEUM.

THAT'S CREEPY.

P-PLEASE, SIR, STOP TRYING TO SCARE ME.

WHAT WAS THAT STRANGE SOUND?

.....

HM ?

CLANK

CLANK

CLANK

AND IT'S ...

CLANK

... GETTING CLOSER.

CLANK

HEAR THAT? IT'S COMING FROM THE BACK OF THE ROOM.

IT CAME FROM THIS ROOM.

SOUNDS INTERESTING, DOESN'T IT? LET'S GO TO THE MUSEUM AND CHECK IT OUT!

HAH...

IT'S BIG NEWS IN THE NEIGHBOR-HOOD!!

YEAH! TWO SECURITY GUARDS SAW IT!!

WHAT? A MEDIEVAL SUIT OF ARMOR WAS WALKING BY ITSELF?

RICHARD MOORE P.I.

HUH?

BWA HA HA HA HA

AREN'T YOU A LITTLE KID?

YEAH, RACHEL! ONLY A LITTLE KID WOULD FALL FOR THAT!

BUT THEY REALLY SAW IT.

YOU'RE STILL A GULLIBLE CHILD, RACHEL!

THE MUSEUM MUST HAVE COME UP WITH THAT STORY TO ATTRACT VISITORS.

STOP RIGHT THERE--!!

I'LL START ON MY HOME-WORK.

BETTER GET BACK TO WORK.

SO MANY WONDERFUL PAINTINGS!!

WOW!!

.....

HUM... ♪ HUM... ♪

ER, SURE...

AREN'T YOU TWO GLAD YOU CAME? ♥

WE'RE GOING, AREN'T WE?

YES...

BAM

NO FAIR. SHE ALWAYS DOES THAT TO GET HER OWN WAY.

YOU BET.

WHY'D I EVER LET HER TAKE KARATE!?

8

HUH?

SO... YOU LIKE THAT PIECE, YOUNG LADY?

WOW! WHAT BEAUTIFUL COLORS!

IT'S NOT TERRIBLY WELL KNOWN, BUT I LIKE THE WARM TOUCH AND THE PIERCING CLARITY OF HIS WORK.

IT'S TITLED "THE ANGELS REST." IT'S ONE OF PICASSI'S MASTER-PIECES.

I LOVE *ALL* THE ARTWORK IN THE MUSEUM.

IT'S NOT ONLY *HIS* WORK ...

OH, NO NEED FOR ALARM. I'M NOT A SHADY CHARACTER.

UH, DO YOU WANT SOMETHING FROM MY DAUGHTER?

I SEE ...

THEY'RE LIKE MY CHILDREN.

9

CLUNK

!?

THE CURATOR!!

NO WONDER YOU KNOW SO MUCH ABOUT THE PAINTINGS!!

MY NAME IS OCHIAI. I AM THE CURATOR OF THIS MUSEUM.

GASP

KUBOTA!! WHAT IN THE WORLD ARE YOU DOING!?

HMPH...

IIJIMA, YOU TAKE CARE OF THIS PIECE.

YOU'RE EXCUSED.

YES, SIR.

I'M ...UH, SORRY.

I'VE TOLD YOU REPEATEDLY TO PUT GLOVES ON BEFORE YOU HANDLE ANYTHING!!

ARE YOU TRYING TO RUIN THE ARTWORK!?

YOU KEEP AT IT 'TIL THEN.

OH WELL. THIS PLACE IS CLOSING IN TEN DAYS ANYWAY.

OH, MR. MANAKA, THE OWNER OF THIS MUSEUM...

AS USUAL, THERE ARE NO PEOPLE IN THIS PLACE.

...ROTTING JUNK!

ENJOY TAKING CARE OF ALL THIS...

UM...

.....

NOW, MR. DESIGNER. THE BLUE-PRINT?

ER, YES...

!?

YES. I BELIEVE DEMOLITION WORK BEGINS NEXT MONTH.

THE MUSEUM IS CLOSING DOWN?

IT'S GOING TO BECOME A BIG HOTEL.

AS SOON AS HE BOUGHT IT, HE STARTED TALKING ABOUT TURNING THIS PLACE INTO A HOTEL!!

MR. MANAKA MADE A PROMISE TO KEEP THE MUSEUM OPEN.

THE PREVIOUS OWNER'S COMPANY WENT BANKRUPT WHEN THE ECONOMIC BUBBLE BURST...

A HOTEL? WHY!?

IIJIMA...

DARN HIM!

THIS MUSEUM HAS A PROUD TRADITION OF FIFTY YEARS, BUT BECAUSE OF THAT MAN...

IT'S ALL H-HIS FAULT.

...SO HE SOLD IT TO THE CURRENT OWNER, MR. MANAKA.

CLANG

THAT GUY IS SO CARELESS...

CLANG CLANG

!?

!?

Y-YES.

HEY, AREN'T YOU KUBOTA?

I'VE HEARD A LOT OF RUMORS ABOUT YOU.

M-MR. MANAKA...

HEY! YOU BE CAREFUL. EVEN JUNK LIKE THAT WILL FETCH A HIGH PRICE WHEN I SELL IT.

......

HA HA HA

YOU BETTER START RAISING MONEY FAST.

PLEASE TAKE YOUR TIME AND ENJOY YOUR VISIT.

HUH?

THERE HE GOES AGAIN...

CLUNK

DARN IT!!

UH, SURE...

CONAN! LET'S GO!!

HE GOT SO ANGRY EARLIER.

THE SEA GALLERY

THE LAND GALLERY

THE HEAVEN GALLERY

HUH?

FORGET IT.

STRANGE... THERE'S SUPPOSED TO BE ANOTHER ROOM PAST HERE.

LET'S HURRY UP AND FINISH OUR TOUR.

KEEP OUT?

keep out

Medieval Art Exhibit

I'M BEAT.

PHEWWWW!

FUNNY. IT WAS OFF LIMITS BEFORE.

HEY. THE SIGN'S GONE.

YOU GUYS ARE PATHETIC.

WE'RE HUNGRY.

C'MON, RACHEL. LET'S GO HOME.

RUMBLE

NO FAIR!!

BUT THE TWO OF YOU CAN COOK YOUR OWN DINNERS!

FINE. GO ON HOME...

HA HA

NO ....!

WE MIGHT AS WELL CHECK OUT THE LAST ROOM TOO!

AFTER HEAVEN, LAND, AND SEA, THE NEXT ONE WILL BE...

LET'S SEE...

WHAT DO YOU THINK THE NEXT ROOM IS LIKE?

THE HELL GALLERY

VWEEEN

VWEEEN

WOW !!

WH- WHAT A DIMLY LIT ROOM.

IT IS THE HELL GALLERY, AFTER ALL.

WHAT A HUGE PAINTING!!

IT'S A HELLISH SCENE, ALL RIGHT.

LET'S SEE. IT'S TITLED "THE WRATH OF HEAVEN"!!

The Wrath of Heaven

INTER-ESTING...

?

IT SAYS IT SHOWS A KNIGHT OF JUSTICE ENTRAPPING A DEMON!

PLISH

HUH?

OH...

OH...

M-MR. MANAKA...

THAT'S RIGHT! OF COURSE I HAVEN'T LET ANYBODY TOUCH THE BODY YET, INSPECTOR MEGUIRE!!

JEEZ... ONCE AGAIN YOU ARE THE FIRST TO DISCOVER THE CRIME.

CAN WE FIND OUT?

M-MAYBE THE SECURITY CAMERA CAUGHT IT!!

YES! WE ALWAYS RECORD IT ONTO VIDEOTAPE.

THERE WERE NO WITNESSES.

ANYBODY SEE THE PERPETRATOR?

!?

HEH HEH... WHAT A FOOL NOT TO REALIZE HE WAS BEING FILMED.

SECURITY ROOM

THERE IT IS, CAPTURED ON TAPE.

HUH?

ONCE I GET A GOOD LOOK AT YOUR FACE I'LL—

NOW SHOW YOURSELF, MURDERER!!

HE APPEARS TO BE LOOKING FOR SOMEBODY.

D-1

THERE'S MR. MANAKA.

D-2

IT LOOKS FAMILIAR ...

THIS SCENE ...

... WAIT A SEC ...

WHAT A FLASHY MURDER.

ONE THRUST TO THE THROAT.

BEEP

AH !!

IT'S EXACTLY LIKE THE PAINTING THAT'S IN FRONT OF THE BODY!!!

ARE YOU SURE?

YES! THE PAINTING'S CALLED "THE WRATH OF HEAVEN"!!

!?

IF ANY VISITORS SAW HIM IN THAT GETUP, THERE'D HAVE BEEN A COMMOTION.

HOW BOLD.

THE MURDERER MUST HAVE KILLED HIM IN IMITATION OF THAT PAINTING.

BUT WHEN WE WENT BACK JUST AFTER 5 P.M., IT WAS GONE.

UH-HUH...

RACHEL! THAT WAS AROUND 4 P.M., RIGHT?

COME TO THINK OF IT, THE CORRIDOR TO THE ROOM WHERE THE CRIME TOOK PLACE WAS BLOCKED WITH A "KEEP OUT" SIGN!!

WHAT!?

keep out

THE MURDERER MUST'VE PUT THE SIGN THERE.

HMM... ACCORDING TO THE DISPLAY ON THE VIDEO THE CRIME OCCURRED AROUND 4:30.

25

THE MURDERER HAD ACCESS TO THE SIGN AND THE ARMOR, AS WELL AS A GOOD KNOWLEDGE OF THE LAYOUT AT THE CRIME SCENE. THAT SUGGESTS IT WAS SOMEONE FROM THE MUSEUM.

THEN HE STABBED MR. MANAKA, WHO HE HAD PREVIOUSLY CALLED TO THE ROOM.

AFTER PLACING THE SIGN IN THE CORRIDOR TO KEEP PEOPLE AWAY, HE PUT ON THE ARMOR AND HID INSIDE THE ROOM.

.....

WHICH MEANS IT WAS ONE OF YOU!

MM?

SEE, THE MURDERER FELL FORWARD AFTER THE FIRST ATTACK. AND THAT'S WHEN ...

WHO GAVE YOU PERMISSION TO REWIND THE TAPE!?

HUH?

HEY, LOOK AT THIS! MR. MANAKA IS DOING SOMETHING.

WHIRRR

NOW HE'S GETTING A PEN FROM THE DESK.

HE'S TAKING A SIGN OFF THE WALL.

... HE JUST REALIZED SOMETHING.

YES! IT LOOKS LIKE ...

HE'S WRITING SOME- THING !!!

HEY !!

HE CRUMPLED IT UP.

THE PAPER ...

H-HE THREW THE PEN AWAY ...

... IN MR. MANAKA'S HANDS ?

COULD IT STILL BE ...

GOOD!

THIS PIECE OF PAPER WAS IN THE VICTIM'S HAND.

THE HELL GALLERY

HEY...

HERE IT IS!

NOBODY BESIDES US, SIR!

NOBODY HAS COME NEAR THE BODY, RIGHT?

!?

KUBOTA!?

Kubota

KU--

HEH HEH HEH. YOU MAY HAVE WORN THE ARMOR TO HIDE YOUR IDENTITY FROM THE SECURITY CAMERA...

...BUT THE VICTIM RECOGNIZED YOU AS THE PERPETRATOR.

WHY *MY* NAME...?

WHAT!?

N-NO! IT WASN'T ME!!

MR. MANAKA WROTE THE NAME OF HIS KILLER ON THIS NOTE AS HIS DYING MESSAGE.

Kubota

AND NOBODY TOUCHED IT AFTER THE BODY WAS FOUND EITHER!!

YOU'RE NOT FOOLING ANYBODY!! AS WE SAW ON THE VIDEO, THE MURDERER NEVER TOUCHED THIS PAPER.

W-WAIT A MINUTE...

THEN THAT MEANS NOBODY CAN VERIFY YOUR WHEREABOUTS.

IN THE FIRST PLACE, I DON'T HAVE ANY MOTIVE TO KILL MR. MANAKA.

IT'S TRUE. I DID ORDER HIM TO DO SOMETHING.

... I WAS ALONE IN THE OFFICE WORKING ON SOMETHING MR. OCHIAI ASKED ME TO DO.

ER, AT THAT TIME...

DO YOU HAVE AN ALIBI? WHERE WERE YOU AROUND 4:30, WHEN THE MURDER WAS COMMITTED?

MR. MANAKA WAS AFTER YOU FOR A HUGE SUM OF MONEY IN PUNITIVE DAMAGES!

THE OTHER DAY YOU WERE EXPOSED FOR SECRETLY SELLING OFF MUSEUM ARTWORK.

MR. IIJIMA?

YOU CAN'T COVER THIS UP, MR. KUBOTA.

.....

YES. ORDINARILY HE WOULD HAVE BEEN FIRED BUT MR. OCHIAI SAID THERE WERE ONLY TEN DAYS LEFT ANYWAY...

IS THAT TRUE?

HMPH! NEVER MIND, I HAVE MY MEN LOOKING FOR THAT ARMOR.

I DIDN'T KILL HIM!!

N-NO, THAT HAS NOTHING TO DO WITH IT!!

HOW COULD YOU DO SOMETHING LIKE THIS!?

AHA!

OH... NOTHING.

WHAT ARE YOU DOING, CONAN?

.....

ONCE IT'S FOUND, THE FACTS WILL BE EVEN CLEARER.

GOOD JOB, KID !!

OH !!

Beika Museum 50th Anniversary

HEY MISTER, THERE'S A PEN HERE!!

WHAT !?

WE HAD THOSE PENS MADE THIS YEAR FOR THE MUSEUM'S FIFTIETH ANNIVERSARY.

OH ...

HMM ... THIS PEN ...

SCRIBBLE SCRIBBLE

SOMEBODY MUST HAVE LEFT IT ON THE DESK.

CLICK

ANYBODY WHO WORKS HERE WOULD HAVE ONE.

11

......

YES, SIR !

SEND THIS TO THE CRIME LAB LATER !!

IT'S PROBABLY THE PEN THE VICTIM USED.

HMM. THE COLOR AND THICKNESS MATCH THE WRITING ON THE DEATH NOTE.

WHY CHOOSE TO COMMIT A CRIME IN A ROOM WHERE HE'D HAVE TO WEAR ARMOR TO HIDE HIS IDENTITY?

MR. KUBOTA WORKS HERE AT THE MUSEUM. HE MUST HAVE KNOWN ABOUT THE SECURITY CAMERAS.

SOMETHING'S STRANGE.

WOULD SOMEONE WITHOUT INTEREST IN ART GO TO SO MUCH TROUBLE TO IMITATE A PAINTING?

JUDGING FROM HIS BEHAVIOR THIS AFTERNOON, HE SEEMS NOT TO CARE ABOUT ARTWORK.

BUT...

WAS IT TO IMITATE THAT PAINTING?

AND NOBODY'S TAMPERED WITH THAT NOTE SINCE THEN.

THE VIDEO CAPTURED THE VICTIM WRITING THAT NOTE.

STILL, THAT DEATH NOTE IS SUCH STRIKING EVIDENCE.

THERE'S GOT TO BE SOMETHING MORE TO THIS CASE!

BUT SOMETHING STILL BOTHERS ME.

SHOO, SHOO. HURRY UP AND GO HOME, KID!!

YOU'RE THE KID FROM MR. MOORE'S ...

HEY, LET'S SEE THAT PART AGAIN!

THE SECURITY ROOM

IT'S LIKE A SPLATTER FLICK ...

WOW! AMAZING!

WHOA!

JUST ONCE, OKAY ...?

WHIRRR

OKAY!

W-WAIT, KID ...

FINE THEN! I'LL TELL THE INSPECTOR HIS POLICEMEN WERE HAVING FUN WATCHING THAT VIDEO.

33

WHAT IS THAT EX-PRESSION !?

WHAT IS THAT !?

R-ROLL THAT PART AGAIN !!!

HUH?

IF IT MADE A SOUND, THE MURDERER WOULD NOTICE ...

AND WHY DID HE THROW THE PEN AWAY AFTER HE FINISHED WRITING!?

... THE POINT OF THE PEN WAS RETRACTED !!!

Beika Museum 50th Anniv...

W-WAIT A SECOND! WHEN I FOUND THE PEN AT THE CRIME SCENE ...

I'VE GOT AN IDEA!

?

!?

IT DOESN'T SEEM NATURAL THAT A PERSON ABOUT TO BE KILLED WOULD BOTHER TO RETRACT A PEN.

STRANGE ...

!?

TAKE CARE OF THE PEN AND THE DEATH NOTE!!

THE HELL GALLERY

WHERE'VE YOU BEEN, CONAN?

UH...

GRAB

HUH?

HEY!!

I WAS RIGHT.

Kubota

THESE MARKS...

!?

I FIGURED THE TRICK OUT!!

YOU FOUND IT !?

INSPECTOR!! WE FOUND THE ARMOR IN MR. KUBOTA'S LOCKER!!

HEY!! WHAT DO YOU THINK YOU'RE DOING !?

AGH !!

THAT'S WRONG!! HE'S NOT THE MURDERER !!

NO ...

SO YOU *ARE* THE MURDERER, MR. KUBOTA.

NO ...

SOMEONE SET UP A CLEVER TRICK WITH THE DEATH NOTE AND THE VIDEO.

THAT SOMEONE IS THE TRUE SUSPECT !!!

FILE 3:
OUT OF INK

THIS IS A MISTAKE !!

IT WASN'T ME !!

THEN WHY WAS THIS BLOODY SUIT OF ARMOR FOUND IN YOUR LOCKER?

I DIDN'T KILL MR. MANAKA !!

... BECAUSE YOU ARE THE MURDERER !!

THE ANSWER IS SIMPLE.

IT WAS THERE ...

I ... I ...

YOU WORE THE ARMOR TO HIDE YOUR IDENTITY FROM THE SECURITY CAMERA!!

YOU CALLED MR. MANAKA TO THIS ROOM, THEN LAY IN WAIT FOR HIM. WHEN HE ARRIVED YOU STABBED HIM TO DEATH.

THE TAPE SHOWED MR. MANAKA WRITING ON THIS SIGN FROM THE WALL WHILE YOUR BACK WAS TURNED.

Kubota

BUT THE CAMERA CLEARLY CAUGHT ANOTHER BIT OF EVIDENCE.

IN OTHER WORDS, THE VICTIM WROTE HIS ATTACKER'S NAME ON THIS DEATH NOTE BEFORE HE WAS KILLED!!

NOBODY TOUCHED IT AFTER THE BODY WAS FOUND, EITHER!

JUDGING FROM THE VIDEO, THE MURDERER NEVER TOUCHED THIS PAPER.

M-MR. OCHIAI...

KUBOTA, I ASKED YOU TO DO SOME WORK BUT I NEVER ASKED YOU TO KILL MR. MANAKA.

LIKE I SAID... I WAS ALONE IN THE OFFICE DOING SOMETHING MR. OCHIAI ASKED ME TO WORK ON.

ON TOP OF THIS, YOU HAVE NO ALIBI.

NO!!

B-BUT I...

...TO PROTECT THEM FROM BEING SPLATTERED BY BLOOD.

THE MURDERER MUST HAVE REMOVED THEM EARLIER...

THERE ARE SIGNS ON THE WALL TO IDENTIFY PAINTINGS, BUT THE PAINTINGS THEMSELVES AREN'T THERE!

THIS CRIME BEARS THE MARK OF SOMEONE WITH A STRONG INTEREST IN ART.

ALSO, THIS PERSON CHOSE A METHOD THAT IMITATED "THE WRATH OF HEAVEN."

ONE OF THESE PEOPLE HERE KILLED MR. MANAKA AND PLAYED A TRICK THAT WOULD FRAME MR. KUBOTA.

THAT SEEMS TO CONFIRM THAT THE MURDERER IS A MUSEUM INSIDER.

...WAS THE MAN WHO ORDERED HIM TO WORK IN THE OFFICE.

THE ONLY ONE WHO COULD ENSURE THAT...

THE TRICK WOULD ONLY WORK IF MR. KUBOTA HAD NO ALIBI!!

W-WAIT!

...NO PROOF THAT THE CURATOR DID IT.

BUT THERE'S NO PROOF...

IT MUST BE THE CURATOR !!!

MR. KUBOTA... YOU'LL COME DOWN TO THE STATION WITH US.

BUT...

N-NO! I CAN'T LET THEM.

...THE MURDERER MIGHT STILL HAVE A CERTAIN PIECE OF EVIDENCE.

IF MY THEORY IS RIGHT...

INHALE

HEY...

ALL RIGHT, IT'S NOW OR NEVER.

THIS IS MY ONLY CHANCE TO FIND OUT !!

I GOTTA GO NOW!!!

I GOTTA GO! I GOTTA GO!!

HUH?

AAAGH, I GOTTA GO PEE!!

TAKE A LEFT OUT OF THIS ROOM, GO DOWN THE STAIRS, THEN--

MISTER, WHERE'S THE BATHROOM?

SO WHEN YOU LEAVE THIS ROOM...

HURRY!

S-SURE...

I CAN'T REMEMBER ALL THAT. WRITE IT DOWN HERE!!

HM?

!?

WHAT'S WRONG? WHY AREN'T YOU WRITING?

DOES THAT PEN HAPPEN TO BE OUT OF INK?

...SO YOU MUST ALREADY KNOW THE PEN DOESN'T WORK.

OH! YOU HAVEN'T EVEN TRIED IT...

THIS CHILD!

BUT THAT'S WEIRD, MISTER. WHY DO YOU HAVE A PEN YOU KNOW YOU CAN'T WRITE WITH?

... SHOULD BE BLANK.

HUH ...?

WAIT A SECOND. IF THE PEN MR. MANAKA USED DIDN'T WORK, THIS DEATH NOTE...

YES, YES.

A PEN YOU CAN'T WRITE WITH?

A PEN ...

LIKE SCRATCHES MADE BY A PEN OUT OF INK.

Kubota

SEE? ON TOP OF THE LETTERS.

MM?

HEY! THERE ARE STRANGE MARKS ON IT!

!?

OOH! IT'S AS IF SOMEONE WAS TRYING TO USE A PEN THAT'S OUT OF INK TO SCRATCH OUT WHAT WAS ALREADY WRITTEN! ♡

WHAT!?

THIS HAD ALREADY BEEN WRITTEN BY THE MURDERER!!

AHA!! SO MR. MANAKA DIDN'T WRITE THIS!!

"LOOK AT THE SIGN BEHIND YOU! THE NAME OF YOUR KILLER IS WRITTEN ON IT!"

I BET THIS IS WHAT THE MURDERER SAID!!

HEH HEH. THAT IS SURPRISINGLY SIMPLE.

BUT WHY WOULD THE OWNER REACH FOR THAT SIGN?

WHAT!?

IS THERE A POSSIBILITY... THAT THE MURDERER SWITCHED PENS?

HEY, WASN'T THAT PEN RETRACTED WHEN IT WAS FOUND?

OH YEAH, I GUESS SO.

!?

I-INDEED...

WHY WOULD SOMEBODY WHO IS ABOUT TO BE KILLED BOTHER TO RETRACT A PEN?

DON'T YOU THINK IT'S STRANGE!?

...HE NEGLECTED TO CLICK THE POINT OF THE PEN OUT FIRST!!

WHEN THE MURDERER SWITCHED THIS WORKING PEN WITH THE DRY PEN...

THAT MEANS THE CULPRIT IS SOMEBODY WHO HAS A PEN THAT'S OUT OF INK.

IN OTHER WORDS...

THE BODY WAS PINNED UP AGAINST THE WALL IN SUCH A SHOWY MANNER.

PEOPLE WHO HEARD THE OUTCRIES CAME RUNNING, BUT THEY ALL HAD THEIR EYES GLUED TO THE BODY!!

THERE WAS PLENTY OF OPPORTUNITY FOR HIM TO MAKE THE SWITCH!!

YOU MUST HAVE DONE IT.

MR. OCHIAI THE CURATOR...

WHERE WERE YOU AT 4:30 AROUND THE TIME OF THE CRIME?

LET'S HEAR YOUR ALIBI!

M-MR. OCHIAI...

I WAS WAITING FOR A CERTAIN SOME-ONE...

AT 4:30...

!?

... WAITING FOR THAT FILTHY DEMON OF AN OWNER.

I WAS IN THIS ROOM, HIDDEN IN A SUIT OF ARMOR ...

IT WASN'T A COINCIDENCE.

THE CAMERA CAPTURED THE SCENE QUITE NICELY FOR YOU.

HMPH ...

THE REST, MR. DETECTIVE, IS EXACTLY AS YOU SAID.

MANY TIMES ?

I PRACTICED MANY TIMES IN THIS ROOM, RECORDING IT ON VIDEO.

THE TIMING OF MY FALL, THE OWNER'S ACTIONS IN THE MEANTIME, THE LOCATION OF THE SIGN, THE PLACEMENT OF THE PEN, MR. MANAKA'S PERSONALITY ...

WAS THAT ACTUALLY YOU ?

THE RUMORS FROM THE SECURITY GUARDS ABOUT AN ARMORED KNIGHT WALKING AROUND LATE AT NIGHT ...

EVEN THE WAY IT WOULD APPEAR ON CAMERA. IT WAS ALL CALCULATED.

HE WAS A DEMON WHO WAS GOING TO DESTROY THIS SACRED MUSEUM FOR HIS OWN PERSONAL PROFIT. THE WORKS OF ART HERE ARE LIKE MY DEAR CHILDREN, AND HE TRIED TO TAKE THEM FROM ME.

YES... I KNEW IT WAS FOOLISH, BUT IT WAS ALL DONE TO SEND THAT MAN TO HIS GRAVE.

.....

I WANTED TO PUNISH YOU, TOO.

AND KUBOTA, YOU STOLE ARTWORK AND SOLD IT OFF.

NO, IT IS EXACTLY LIKE THE PAINTING.

BUT UNLIKE THE PAINTING, YOU ALSO WILL KNOW THE WRATH OF HEAVEN.

HMPH. THAT'S WHY YOU FRAMED MR. KUBOTA...

...AND GAVE THE OWNER A TASTE OF "THE WRATH OF HEAVEN."

...THE STORY OF THAT PAINTING?

DO YOU KNOW...

THE KNIGHT OF JUSTICE DID INDEED SLAY THE DEMON, BUT HE WAS SPLATTERED WITH THE EVIL BLOOD ...

... AND EVENTUALLY TURNED EVIL HIMSELF.

WHATEVER MY REASONS, I AM NOW A MURDERER.

I TOO ... HAVE BECOME LIKE A DEMON.

AS PROOF, I COULD NOT DECEIVE THE PURE YOUNG EYES OF JUSTICE.

YOUNG EYES OF JUSTICE?

.....

HA HA HA ...

MY BOY... DIDN'T YOU HAVE TO GO TO THE BATHROOM?

OH! UH ...

HEH ...

Richard Moore Does it Again!
Great Detective solves tough case!

NOW I'M FAMOUS!!

LOOK! LOOK! THERE'S A BIG PIECE ON IT!!

HEY!

YEAH. BECAUSE OF THE INCIDENT, THE COMMUNITY RALLIED TO SAVE IT.

WOW. SO THE MUSEUM'S GOING TO STAY OPEN.

THE GREAT DETECTIVE RICHARD MOORE!!

AND IT'S ALL BECAUSE I SOLVED THE CASE!!

WHAT'S A GUY TO DO!?

HAAA HA HA

52

VWOOSH

REALLY!

BZZZ

YEAH RIGHT! I FOUND YOU DRUNK, PASSED OUT AT THE FRONT DOOR.

WHAT AM I SUPPOSED TO DO? MY MEETING WITH A CLIENT RAN LATE INTO THE NIGHT AND I OVERSLEPT.

AW, BE QUIET!

NORMAL PEOPLE DON'T SHAVE ON THE TRAIN ON THEIR WAY TO THEIR FRIEND'S WEDDING.

CLACKITY CLACK

YEAH, YEAH...

TUG

GROWN UPS HAVE THEIR OWN WAY OF DOING THINGS.

UH
...

YEAH!

YOU WANTED TO GO TO KYOTO TOO, DIDN'T YOU, CONAN?

IT'S BECAUSE THE WEDDING IS IN KYOTO. I'VE NEVER BEEN THERE BEFORE!

HMPH. I BROUGHT YOU ALONG BECAUSE YOU BEGGED ME!

NO
...

JEEZ... STILL NO WORD FROM HIS PARENTS?

UH-OH
...

WE COULDN'T JUST LEAVE HIM IN TOKYO.

WHY'S HE HERE, ANYWAY?

RATTLE

THEY'RE THE ONES WHO FED ME THE POISON THAT MADE ME SMALL.

THIS IS ALL THOSE GUYS' FAULT.

IT'S NOT LIKE I LIKE LIVING WITH YOU GUYS, EITHER.

I-I'M GOING TO THE BATHROOM.

DASH

55

THEY DON'T KNOW THE DRUG MADE ME SMALL.

THAT'S RIGHT...

HMPH! DARN BRAT...

MOVE! YOU'RE IN THE WAY!!

WHAT!?

IT'S THE PERFECT OPPORTUNITY TO STEAL THAT DRUG FROM THEM.

THIS IS MY CHANCE!!

...HIGH SCHOOL DETECTIVE JIMMY KUDO...

ONCE I'M BACK AS...

...AND THEN...

ONCE WE FIND OUT THE INGREDIENTS OF THAT DRUG, DOC CAN FIND A WAY TO GET ME BACK TO NORMAL...

COUNT ON IT!!!

...I'LL REVEAL ALL YOUR EVIL DOINGS!!

WHAT ARE THEY DOING HERE!?

BUT THOSE GUYS...

VWOOOSH

WHERE ARE THEY GOING?

RATTLE

SHUFF

!?

ARE THEY MEETING SOMEBODY!?

GLANCE GLANCE

THE DINING CAR!?

UP-STAIRS?

GRAB

HUH?

...THEIR BOSS?

C-COULD IT BE...

BA-BUMP

BA-BUMP

WHO COULD IT BE...?

BA-BUMP

BA-BUMP

BUT YOU JUST ATE LUNCH!

I-I'M HUNGRY.

HEY! WHAT ARE YOU DOING IN HERE!?

R-RACHEL...

UH... WAIT...

C'MON! DON'T GIVE ME ANY TROUBLE.

...AND PUT IT AROUND THE BUG THAT DOC GAVE ME.

TUP

CHEW CHEW

...CHEW SOME GUM...

CHOMP

RATS! GUESS I'LL HAVE TO...

...UNDER THEIR SEAT.

TMP

...AND STICK IT HERE...

SHFF

I JUST ROLL IT UP...

SQUEEZE

60

NOW WHAT'RE YOU DOING!?

BA-BUMP

ALWAYS WRAP IT IN PAPER FIRST. THEN INTO THE ASHTRAY!

G-GIVE IT BACK.

CHAK

YOU SHOULDN'T BE DOING STUFF LIKE THIS!!

REALLY! STICKING GUM UNDER THE SEAT!

HEE HEE ♥ ...

GLARE

REALLY ...

SHFF

O-KAY ...

GOT IT!?

HOPE THEY DON'T FIND IT ...

OH WELL. AT LEAST IT'S IN THE ASHTRAY.

DRAG

DRAG

OH! THEY'RE BACK!!

RATTLE

"YOU CAN HEAR EVERY-THING WITH THESE GLASSES!!"

"IF YOU ADJUST THE DIAL TO THE RIGHT FREQUENCY, A SPECIAL SOUND WAVE WILL STIMULATE YOUR EARDRUM."

"THE RIGHT SIDE OF YOUR GLASSES IS FOR THE BUG, THE LEFT IS FOR THE EARPHONE!!"

LET'S SEE... TO PICK UP THE SOUNDS FROM THE BUG...

UH-OH!

WHAT IS IT !?

HM? THERE'S SOME-THING IN HERE.

I HEAR THEM!

PHEW. I CAN FINALLY HAVE A SMOKE !!

THAT WAS CLOSE.

PHEW

A PREVIOUS PASSENGER MUST'VE PUT IT IN HERE.

IT'S JUST GUM.

THEY HAD A BLACK ATTACHÉ CASE WHEN THEY WERE IN THE DINING CAR.

THEY DON'T HAVE IT ANY-MORE.

HM? SOME-THING'S DIFFERENT.

INSTEAD THEY HAVE THAT LARGE SUIT-CASE.

COULD THAT MEAN ...?

DON'T WORRY. NOBODY'S LISTENING.

SHH! LOWER YOUR VOICE, KASPAR!!

I KNEW IT ...

THAT WAS AN EASY DEAL.

MELKIOR AND KASPAR?

HA HA HA... YOU'RE ALWAYS SO CAUTIOUS, MELKIOR.

ARE THOSE CODE-NAMES!!?

MONEY?

INFORMATION CONCERNING MONEY.

FLICK

WHAT WAS INSIDE THAT CASE?

TAP TAP

¥400 MILLION JUST FOR HANDING THAT BLACK CASE OVER.

YEAH, THE CONTACT MUST BE SITTING BACK, CHUCKLING AND LOOKING DOWN AT THE SCENERY.

I SEE. THAT'S WHY THE CONTACT WAS SO HAPPY.

IF THEY USE THAT INFORMATION, ¥400 MILLION IS GONNA BE CHUMP CHANGE.

THAT CONTACT IS NO LONGER VALUABLE TO THE SYNDICATE.

LAST...?

A GOOD LAST LOOK.

A STRONG SHOCK WILL TRIGGER THE BOMB AND MAKE IT GO OFF.

!?

THE BLACK CASE WE HANDED OVER CONTAINED EXPLOSIVES.

NO... THAT'S WHEN OUR FRIEND WILL UNKNOWINGLY TRIGGER THE SWITCH.

IT'S A TIME BOMB !?

DON'T WORRY. AFTER FINALLY GETTING AHOLD OF THIS VALUABLE INFORMATION, THE CONTACT'S GOING TO TREAT IT WITH KID GLOVES.

BUT... WHAT IF THE CONTACT WERE TO DROP THAT CASE RIGHT NOW?

BUT THE EXPLOSION *WILL* OCCUR AT 3:10.

WHAT !?

...WILL BE *EIGHTY-SIXED!*

TEN SECONDS AND THE TRAIN WILL BE BLOWN TO BITS AND OUR CONTACT ...

HEH HEH HEH ... ONCE THE SWITCH IS TRIGGERED, IT'S ALL OVER.

!?

EIGHTY-SIXED!?

UH, RIGHT...?

HMPH! LITTLE BRAT GAVE ME A SCARE...

AND TEN TIME TEN IS A HUNDRED...

OH, YEAH!

NO, IT'S EIGHTY-ONE.

HUH?

NINE TIMES NINE IS EIGHTY-SIX!!

NO ...

HEY! LET'S GET OUTTA HERE.

WE ARE NOW ARRIVING AT NAGOYA STATION ...

ATTENTION LADIES AND GENTLEMEN ...

HEY ...

DASH

W-WAIT !!

... I NEED TO FIND OUT FROM YOU!

... A TON OF THINGS ...

THERE ARE STILL ...

I CAN'T TAKE MY EYES OFF YOU FOR A SECOND!

NO ...

HEY!

THEN THE PERSON THEY HAD THE DEAL WITH MUST STILL BE ON BOARD.

WAIT A SEC. THEY SAID THEY WERE PLANNING ON DESTROYING THIS TRAIN.

IF I DON'T FIND THAT PERSON BY THEN, WE COULD ALL ...

DAMN IT! ONLY FORTY MINUTES 'TIL 3:10!!

THERE ARE HUNDREDS OF PASSENGERS ON BOARD!

BUT HOW CAN I DO THAT!?

FILE 5: FOUR PEOPLE IN FIRST CLASS

THE BOMB GOES OFF AT 3:10 !!

VWOOSH

...MUST HAVE THE BLACK CASE WITH THE BOMB INSIDE!

WHOEVER MADE THE DEAL WITH THE MEN IN BLACK ...

I HAVE TO FIND THE BOMB BY THEN!!

ONLY 38 MINUTES LEFT.

I HAVE TO FIND IT !!

I'D BETTER HURRY UP AND FIND THE PERSON HOLDING THE BLACK CASE WITH THE BOMB.

IT'S NO USE. THEY WON'T BELIEVE ME.

ON THE OTHER HAND, I DON'T HAVE ANY OTHER LEADS.

IT'D BE IMPOSSIBLE TO CHECK THEM ALL OUT IN TIME.

BUT THERE ARE TONS OF PEOPLE WITH BLACK CASES.

WAIT A SECOND ...

... DINING CAR?

RATS! IF ONLY RACHEL HADN'T GOTTEN IN MY WAY...

...I WOULD'VE SEEN THE FACE OF THE PERSON THEY WERE WAITING FOR IN THE DINING CAR.

"PHEW..."

WHEN THEY CAME BACK AFTER FINISHING THEIR DEAL...

THE DINING CAR IS NOT A NON-SMOKING CAR!! HE COULD HAVE SMOKED AS MUCH AS HE WANTED.

WH-WHAT COULD THAT MEAN?

!?

"I CAN FINALLY HAVE A SMOKE."

...MUST HAVE DISLIKED BEING AROUND SMOKE.

I'VE GOT IT! THE PERSON THEY WERE DEALING WITH...

...IS SITTING IN A NON-SMOKING CAR!!!

THAT SUGGESTS THE PERSON THEY WERE DEALING WITH, THAT IS TO SAY, THE PERSON WHO RECEIVED THE BOMB...

EIGHT!!!

HOW MANY NON-SMOKING CARS ARE THERE?

IF I ONLY KNEW THE CAR THE PERSON IS RIDING IN.

BUT THAT ONLY NARROWS IT DOWN TO EIGHT OUT OF SIXTEEN CARS-- STILL TOO MANY.

"INFOR-MATION CON-CERNING MONEY."

"WHAT WAS INSIDE THAT CASE?"

"¥400 MILLION YEN JUST FOR HANDING THAT BLACK CASE OVER."

THINK! THERE'S GOTTA BE SOMETHING ELSE--A CLUE IN THEIR CONVER-SATION.

L-LOOKING DOWN !?

"... LOOKING DOWN AT THE SCENERY."

"YEAH, THE CONTACT MUST BE SITTING BACK, CHUCKLING, AND..."

"I-I SEE. THAT'S WHY THE CONTACT WAS SO HAPPY."

OUT OF THOSE, WHICH ARE NON-SMOKING ?

THERE ARE THREE FIRST CLASS CARS.

YOU CAN ONLY LOOK DOWN AT THE SCENERY IF YOU'RE IN ONE OF THE FIRST CLASS CARS ON THE SECOND FLOOR!!

IT'S THE ONLY ONE!!

CAR 7 ON THE SECOND FLOOR!!

2F

1F

VWOOSH

OF COURSE HE'S IN FIRST CLASS--HE'S A BIG SHOT THAT CAN COME UP WITH ¥400 MILLION.

CAR 7, 2ND FLOOR (1ST CLASS)

...MUST BE HERE !!

THE PERSON WITH THE BLACK CASE AND THE BOMB...

I'M SURE OF IT.

AND IF THE BIG SHOT HATES SMOKE, THIS CAR IS THE LOGICAL CHOICE.

WHOA! HE'S GOT A GOLD ROLEX ON HIS WRIST.

TAP TAP

THE LAPTOP SCREEN SHOWS STOCK TRADING INFORMATION.

I'LL START WITH THE BUSINESS-MAN.

THE BLACK CASE IS ON HIS KNEES, UNDER HIS LAPTOP.

ALL RIGHT...

THIS GUY MUST BE MAKING A KILLING IN STOCKS.

LIAR! THE CIRCLES AND SQUARES ARE ALL LINED UP!

THIS IS *NOT* A TOY.

TAP TAP

MM?

HEY MISTER! LEMME PLAY THAT GAME!

B A M

HEY!

FWISH

THEN CAN I PLAY WITH THIS BLACK ONE? THIS IS A GAME TOO, RIGHT?

MEANIE!

I HAVE WORK TO DO!! GO AWAY!

78

OH. THE SECOND PROSPECT ...

WHAT'S WRONG, LITTLE BOY? ARE YOU LOST?

PESKY KID ...

OW!!

THE SMALL BAG HAS A CELL PHONE INSIDE.

AN ENGLISH NEWSPAPER IN HAND, A CAN OF JUICE AND A SMALL BAG ON THE TABLE.

WOW, THAT'S COOL!!

DASH

ALL RIGHT ...

THE BLACK CASE IS ON THE WINDOW SEAT.

YOU LIKE MT. FUJI?

OH BOY, MT. FUJI!?

Y-YEAH!

JIGGLE JIGGLE

YOU CAN GET A PERFECT VIEW OF MT. FUJI!

MMM, IT'S NICE AND CLEAR TODAY.

WHAT A GREAT VIEW!!

YANK

HEY! KEEP IT DOWN, KID!!

DIDN'T I TELL YOU TO BUZZ OFF!?

AGH

DARN! IT'S LOCKED.

HUH? WHY?

...

EXCUSE ME, MA'AM. WERE YOU IN THE DINING CAR?

DARN ...

NOW SHOO!

M-MY MISTAKE!

THAT MUST'VE BEEN SOMEBODY ELSE! I HAVEN'T BEEN TO THE DINING CAR.

YOU LOOK A LOT LIKE THE LADY WHO WAS WITH THE GUYS DRESSED IN BLACK BACK AT THE DINING CAR.

YIKES.

... TO GO TO A PLACE LIKE THAT!!

I AM WAY TOO BUSY ...

MISTER, DID YOU GO TO THE DINING CAR?

80

HOW AM I GOING TO CHECK IT OUT?

HE'S HOLDING THE BLACK CASE SECURELY IN HIS ARMS.

HE'S LISTENING TO SOMETHING ON HIS WALKMAN.

NOW FOR THE THIRD PERSON-- THE STOUT OLD MAN.

SIR ...

DID YOU GO TO THE DINING CAR EARLIER?

EH ?

...

I'LL COME BACK TO THE OLD MAN LATER.

DASH

I NEVER TIRE OF GOING TO DISNEY LAND!!

HOHOHO

THIS IS HOPELESS.

OH, I DID INDEED !!

I SAID, DID YOU GO TO THE DINING CAR!?

LOOKS LIKE I CAN'T GET TO THIS ONE, EITHER.

THE BLACK CASE IS UP THERE ON THE LUGGAGE RACK.

GOLD NECKLACE AND GOLD-RIMMED GLASSES, GOLD RING AND GOLD EARRING. EVERYTHING'S GOLD.

FINALLY THE FOURTH PERSON-- THE YAKUZA GUY.

GLINT

S-SIR, DID YOU GO TO THE DINING ...

IT'S ...

THAT PAPER NAPKIN.

!?

F-FORGET IT ...

HA HA HA...

SQUEAK SQUEAK

J·DINER

82

THIS GUY *WAS* IN THE DINING CAR!!

IT'S THE KIND THEY HAVE AT THE DINING CAR.

JD J-DINER

ALL RIGHT !!!

THANKS!

...

UM... MY PAPER AIRPLANE LANDED UP THERE. CAN I GET IT?

DON'T TOUCH THAT !!

!?

ACK!

CLICK

HMM. WHERE'D IT GO?

I CAN'T FIND IT !!

WHACK

YOU LITTLE--!

SNICKER SNICKER ...

UNDER-WEAR?

LOVE

HUH?

BOINK

YOU'RE SUCH A RASCAL !!

R-RACHEL ...

CONAN !

OW ...

AND DON'T COME BACK !!!

BOOT

NO !!

BUT I STILL NEED TO--

YOU BETTER NOT GET OUT OF LINE AGAIN, OR ELSE!!

THERE'S THREE LEFT!!

I WAS ABLE TO ELIMINATE ONE PERSON.

ONLY FOURTEEN MINUTES LEFT.

DARN IT!!

ONE OF THOSE THREE !!!

ONE OF THEM HAS THE BLACK CASE WITH THE BOMB ...

FILE 6:
TEN SECONDS OF TERROR

VWOOSH

TWELVE MINUTES TO THE EXPLOSION ...

TICK

TICK

TICK

FROM THEIR CONVERSATION, I'VE NARROWED IT DOWN TO ONE OF THREE PEOPLE SITTING ON THE 2ND FLOOR OF CAR SEVEN.

THE EXCHANGE MUST HAVE TAKEN PLACE IN THE DINING CAR!!

THE GUYS IN BLACK EXCHANGED THAT CASE FOR ¥400 MILLION ...

IF I DON'T FIND THE PERSON CARRYING THE BLACK CASE WITH THE BOMB...THIS TRAIN WILL BE BLOWN TO BITS.

89

!?

"THAT'S WHEN OUR FRIEND WILL UNKNOWINGLY TRIGGER THE SWITCH."

SOMETHING WILL TRIGGER THE EXPLOSION!

HEY, THAT MEANS ...

A WALK-MAN ...

A CELL PHONE INSIDE HER BAG ...

A LAP-TOP ...

WAIT A SECOND ... WHAT DID EACH OF THEM HAVE?

I'LL GO BACK TO THEIR CAR AGAIN.

ALL RIGHT ...

I NEED SOME OTHER CLUES.

IT'S NO HELP. ANY OF THOSE THINGS COULD HAVE A TRIGGER MECHANISM.

LIM, BUT I...

DIDN'T I TELL YOU TO SIT STILL?

FWUMP

UH...

HEY! WHERE DO YOU THINK *YOU'RE* GOING, *CONAN!*?

GRAB

YOU JUST WENT TO THE BATH-ROOM.

I HAVE TO PEE.

MAYBE I'LL TAKE A WALK...

GET IT ON OUR RETURN TRIP!!

I WANT A SOUVENIR...

YOU CAN WAIT!

I-I'M THIRSTY...

I SAID NO !!

THERE'S ONLY ONE WAY TO MAKE HER BELIEVE ME!!

BUT WHO'D BELIEVE A KID TELLING A STORY LIKE THIS...?

THERE'S NO CHOICE BUT TO TELL RACHEL EVERYTHING AND EVACUATE ALL THE PASSENGERS !!

N-NO! ONLY SEVEN MINUTES LEFT!!

YOU'RE SUCH A TROUBLE-MAKER.

I'LL TELL RACHEL WHO I REALLY AM!!!

ONCE SHE FINDS OUT I'M JIMMY KUDO, RACHEL WILL BELIEVE WHAT I HAVE TO SAY.

AND IF RACHEL TELLS PEOPLE, THEY'LL BELIEVE HER.

THEN RACHEL AND I ...

B-BUT IF I DO NOTHING ...

AND ALL THE OTHER PASSENGERS ...

BUT... IF THE MEN IN BLACK FIND OUT I'M STILL ALIVE AS A KID, THEY'LL TRY TO KILL ME AGAIN.

IF THAT HAPPENS, RACHEL WILL BE IN DANGER BECAUSE OF HER ASSOCIATION WITH ME.

WE'LL DIE IN THE EXPLOSION ANYWAY!

B L A M

LISTEN UP ...

ER, RACHEL ...

ER ...

CLACKITY CLACK

IT'S NOT POLITE, ESPECIALLY WHEN YOU'RE TALKING TO PEOPLE OLDER THAN YOU.

.....

HEY! DON'T TAKE THAT TONE OF VOICE WITH ME.

KLONK

THERE YOU GO AGAIN ...

YOU MUST LISTEN, RACH ...

THIS IS SERIOUS.

HUH ...?

THEY WERE SITTING ON THE MOUNTAIN SIDE!!

IF SHE HAD BEEN THERE PICKING UP THE CASE WITH THE BOMB, SHE WOULD HAVE HAD A GREAT VIEW!!

THE DINING CAR!!

!?

SHE LIED TO CONCEAL THE TRANSACTION...

"I HAVEN'T BEEN TO THE DINING CAR."

IF SHE HAD CONFUSED THE VIEW SHE HAD AT THE DINING CAR WITH THE VIEW FROM HER OWN SEAT...

ATTENTION LADIES AND GENTLEMEN. AS A COURTESY TO OTHERS, PASSENGERS WISHING TO USE CELLULAR PHONES...

THERE'S ONLY THIRTY SECONDS TO GO!!!

SHE'S THE ONE!!

!?

...ARE REQUESTED TO DO SO ONLY IN THE AREA BETWEEN CARS.

SHE HAS THE BOMB!!!

STOP, CONAN!

IT'S THE CELL PHONE!

DASH

THAT'S IT!!

HEY...

ZHOOP

BEEP

FSHHH

BEEP
BEEP
BEEP

BUT WITH A PHONE...

THAT'S RIGHT. WITH A LAPTOP OR A WALKMAN, THERE'S NO WAY TO MAKE SOMEONE PUSH A SPECIFIC KEY RIGHT AT 3:10.

DASH DASH

THAT'S ALL YOU NEED TO DO !!

YOU JUST SET UP A SPECIFIC TIME AND PHONE NUMBER.

THE BOMB IS PROBABLY SET TO RESPOND TO A DESIGNATED PHONE NUMBER.

CLICK

RRRRRING ...CLICK

SHFF

HELLO ?

HELLO ?

HMM... NOBODY'S PICKING UP...

I'M A DETEC- TIVE !!!

CONAN EDOGAWA !!

WH-WHO ARE YOU ...?

WHEW ...

HUH ?

I-I'M ACTUALLY JUST A FIRST- GRADER.

HA HA HA...

HEY! ARE YOU UP TO NO GOOD AGAIN !?

YANK

D-DETECTIVE?

OF COURSE, THE LOCKED CASE AND THE PHONE CALL AT THE APPOINTED TIME WAS ALL PART OF THE TRAP SET BY THOSE MEN.

THE LADY HAD MADE THE PHONE CALL BECAUSE THE MEN IN BLACK HAD PROMISED TO TELL HER HOW TO UNLOCK THE CASE WHEN SHE CALLED.

BUT IN THE END, NOT A SINGLE PERSON GOT HURT.

THE TRAIN STOPPED, THE POLICE CAME, AND WE WERE LATE FOR THE WEDDING. IT WAS A BIG MESS...

STILL, THIS INCIDENT CLEARED UP A LITTLE BIT OF THAT FOG.

SHE TOLD THE POLICE ALL THIS, BUT IT TURNED OUT SHE HADN'T BEEN SO DEEPLY INVOLVED WITH THE MEN IN BLACK.

IN THE END, THEIR TRUE IDENTITY REMAINED ENSHROUDED IN A THICK FOG.

I WILL NEVER FORGET THOSE NAMES.

KASPAR AND MELKIOR... THOSE ARE THEIR CODENAMES.

I *WILL* TRACK THEM DOWN ...

YOU CAN COUNT ON IT !!!

FILE 7:
GET THE CODE!!

TEITAN ELEMENTARY SCHOOL...

THAT'S WHAT I'VE BEEN TRYING TO TELL YOU!

MM?

AND WHAT'S WITH THIS RACCOON?

THERE'S NO SUCH PLANET.

THERE'S A PLANET CALLED DAITA AND...

YADDA YADDA   YADDA

!

YEAH, LOOK!

CODE?

HEY! LET'S HAVE CONAN CRACK THE CODE.

HI, CONAN!

WHAT'S GOING ON?

WHAT IS THIS CODE FOR?

IT'S TO WIN A KAMEN YAIBA DOLL!!

......

だ" き た
い た て
た み た
せ は ん
い さ
か た
た い
い だ"

KAMEN YAIBA...?

YEAH! MY DAD TOOK ME TO THE KAMEN YAIBA EVENT THEY'RE HAVING AT TOTO TOWER!

THERE WAS THIS SECRET CODE BOOTH, AND THEY SAID IF I FIGURED IT OUT I'D GET A DOLL!

BUT DAD COULDN'T FIGURE IT OUT.

SO YOU ASKED THEM?

JUST READ IT BACK-WARDS! "DAITA-SAN TATETA TANUKI WA MITA, KITA..."

MR. DAITA BUILT RACCOON SAW HEARD...

WHERE DOES IT SAY TO READ IT BACK-WARDS?

ER, WELL...

HEY, CONAN! THIS IS ABOUT PLANET DAITA, RIGHT?

RIGHT?

......

HUH?

"DAI-SEIKA! KIMI WA TENSAI DA!"

CORRECT! YOU ARE A GENIUS!!

NO... THAT'S WHAT IT SAYS ON THE PAPER!

WHAT'D I TELL YOU! HE SAYS I'M RIGHT!

"TANUKI" CAN ALSO MEAN "TAKE OUT TA."

THIS "TANUKI" IS THE KEY.

SEE THE DRAWING OF THE TANUKI RACCOON?

WHAT!?

.....

SEE?

"DAI SEIKA I KI MIWA TE NSA IDA" OR "CORRECT, YOU ARE A GENIUS!"

SO... READ IT WITHOUT THE TA'S!

YOU'RE LIKE KID KOBAYASHI FROM THE JUNIOR DETECTIVE LEAGUE!!

ER, WELL ...

YOU'RE SO SMART !!!

WOW, CONAN !!!

Y-YOU GUYS ...

THEN I SUPPOSE I'LL BE HERCULE POIROT.

I'M SHERLOCK HOLMES!

THEN I'M KOGORO AKECHI!

SAME HERE ...

......

AND MY MOM'S BUSY AT HOME.

MY DAD WON'T TAKE ME BACK A SECOND TIME.

BUT WHO'LL TAKE US?

ALL RIGHT, LET'S ALL GO TO TOTO TOWER ON SATURDAY TO GET THE KAMEN YAIBA DOLL !!

SOMEONE TO TAKE US, HUH?

LISTEN UP, KIDS!

TOTO TOWER

MEET ME BACK HERE AT THE OBSERVATORY AT SIX O'CLOCK, OKAY!?

OKAY!!

RACHEL WAS OUR ONLY OPTION...

LIKE I SAID, SHE'S NOT MY SISTER.

AND QUIT OGLING!

YOUR SISTER HAS BIG BOOBS.

SHE'S NOT MY SISTER.

YOUR BIG SISTER IS PRETTY, CONAN!

ALL RIGHT, LET'S HURRY UP AND GET THE DOLL AND THEN GO CHECK OUT THE KAMEN YAIBA SHOW !!

YEAH

OKAY !!

DON'T GET LOST NOW !!

HOW CUTE. ♡

CHUCKLE

SCAMPER

......

DID I SURPRISE YOU?

CONAN ...?

CO--

UH, NO ...

THAT'S FOR KIDS ...

CONAN, AREN'T YOU GOING TO THE KAMEN YAIBA SHOW?

TH-THANKS ...

HERE, TAKE IT! IT'S FOR YOU!

HEY, WHAT DID YOU MEAN BY "REAL IDENTITY" ...?

......

114

UH-OH...

YOU SAID, "I HAVE TO TELL YOU MY REAL IDENTITY!"

REMEMBER THE OTHER DAY ON THE TRAIN?

HUH?

MY REAL IDENTITY IS...

M-MY...

UH, NO... SEE...

YOU NEVER TOLD ME.

YAA!

HUH?

MY REAL IDENTITY IS KAMEN YAIBA!!

MAYBE I'M THINKING TOO MUCH ...

HA HA HA

VOOM!

BUT SOME-DAY ...

I CAN'T TELL YOU WHO I AM, YET.

I CAN'T DO IT.

I'M SORRY, RACHEL ...

I PROMISE.

SOME-DAY ...

WHAT, YOU LOST THE DOLL!?

BUT WHEN I... WHEN I CAME OUT IT WAS GONE!

UH-HUH. I PUT THE BAG WITH THE DOLL IN IT RIGHT IN FRONT OF THE BATHROOM.

ARE YOU SURE, AMY?

AND THIS BAG WAS THERE INSTEAD.

WHAAT !?

I SEE. SOMEBODY MUST'VE TAKEN IT BY MISTAKE.

...A FLASH-LIGHT.

HMM... A MAP GUIDE, BINOCULARS AND...

HEY ...

CLUNK

LET'S TAKE A LOOK INSIDE THIS BAG!!

SHFF

SOME-THING'S IN IT!

MM ?

MA

UM
...

WHAT'S THIS?

←ORO

OH, SO IT'S YOURS.

HEY! THAT'S MY BAG!!

.....

NO PROBLEM.

I'M SORRY TO HAVE TROUBLED YOU.

I'M SORRY. I WAS IN A RUSH. I MUST HAVE MISTAKEN HER BAG FOR MINE.

THERE YOU ARE, KAMEN YAIBA!!

118

I WANT SUSHI!!

REALLY? I WANT GRILLED EEL!!

I'LL TREAT YOU GUYS TO A SNACK!

HOW ABOUT A FRENCH RESTAURANT?

SHALL WE GET A BITE TO EAT?

BOY, I'M STARVING!

UM...

I SAID A SNACK, DIDN'T I!?

OH...

PAPER?

WAS THERE A SMALL PIECE OF PAPER INSIDE THAT BAG?

SORRY TO TROUBLE YOU AGAIN.

WHAT IS IT NOW?

HEY...

LET ME CHECK...

VWSH

NO...

BUT IT MUST HAVE BEEN IN THERE...

RIGHT!?

HUH?

WE HAVEN'T SEEN IT!!

HUH !

GULP

GASP

I'LL CALL THE POLICE.

IF YOU DON'T GET LOST ...

DASH

SHE'S NOT MY ...

YOUR SISTER IS STRONG, CONAN!

WOW !

DASH

AGHH !!

HEY, WANNA SEE SOME-THING COOL?

?

I'LL BE BACK AROUND EIGHT, I THINK.

UH-HUH. I'M ON MY WAY HOME.

DAD?

HEY!!

TA-DAA!

SEE?

LET ME SEE. YES, THIS LOOKS LIKE SOME KIND OF CODE.

UH, TREA-SURE?

WOW! REALLY?

SHUT UP. I'M THE ONE THAT FOUND THIS TREASURE MAP!!

WHAT!? WHY DIDN'T YOU GIVE IT BACK TO HIM?

121

TREA-SURE, HUH?

YAY!

ALL RIGHT. TOMORROW, WE GO TREASURE HUNTING!!

DINO CAPANE, THE LEADER OF AN ITALIAN GANG OF BURGLARS, WAS CAPTURED HERE IN JAPAN YESTERDAY. AFTER A NIGHT IN JAIL, HE STILL HAS NOT BROKEN HIS SILENCE.

OH, SORRY...

C'MON, CONAN! WE'RE LEAVING!?

THE LOCATION OF THE 15,000 MAPLE LEAF GOLD COINS THE MEN STOLE REMAINS UNKNOWN.

POLICE ARE SEARCHING FOR CAPANE'S PARTNERS, STILL AT LARGE, BUT THEY HAVE NO LEADS ON THEIR WHEREABOUTS.

ONY

FILE 8: THE ABC'S OF CODE CRACKING

BEIKA PARK...

YOU'RE LATE, CONAN!!

SORRY...

NATURALLY.

YUP!

YOU GUYS KEPT MUM TO YOUR PARENTS TOO, RIGHT?

IT TOOK SOME TIME TO SNEAK AWAY FROM RACHEL.

ALL RIGHT, GUYS! LEMME SEE WHAT YOU BROUGHT!!

TREASURE, HUH?

SHFF SHFF

IF OUR PARENTS FIND OUT, THERE'S A RISK THEY MAY CONFISCATE IT.

OUR GOAL IS TO CRACK THIS CODE AND FIND THE TREASURE.

...A SET OF WRITING TOOLS.

I BROUGHT A MAP AND A COMPASS AND...

I BROUGHT OPERA GLASSES SO WE CAN SEE FAR AWAY!!

...TO DIG THE TREASURE UP!!

I BROUGHT A SHOVEL AND LITTLE RAKES...

I BROUGHT THIS, RIGHT HERE.

HOW 'BOUT YOU, CONAN?

THAT'S FINE... THEN YOU CAN...

I-I BROUGHT MY BRAIN...

OH... SO ONCE AGAIN YOU BROUGHT NOTHING?

I'M TALKING ABOUT MY BRAIN!

HUH? IS THERE SOMETHING SPECIAL ABOUT THIS HAT?

WHAT?

BAM

...CARRY EVERYTHING!!

.....

ALL RIGHT! WE'VE GOT THE CODE, SO LET'S GO!!

GIMME A BREAK ...

UM... UH...

WHERE TO ...?

SLIP

HURRAH

HEY, HANG ON.

LOOK CLOSELY AT THE CODE !!

N-NO ...

YOU SAYING YOU KNOW, MITCH!?

HOW SHOULD I KNOW !?

OH !!!

YOU KNOW, THE PLACE WHERE WE FOUND THIS CODE YESTERDAY.

......

HAVEN'T YOU SEEN IT SOME-WHERE?

SEE THIS DIAGRAM AT THE VERY TOP?

126

Destination: Toto Tower

BEEP

HA HA HA ...

THE TREASURE IS AS GOOD AS FOUND!

RIGHT FROM THE START I SUSPECTED IT WAS AT TOTO TOWER.

HEH HEH HEH ...

Destination: Toto Tower

VROOOM...

IT SAYS ORO ...

BUT WHAT DO THESE LETTERS MEAN?

← ORO

I KNOW WHAT IT IS !!

TH-THAT'S IT!

!

COULD IT BE AN ACRONYM?

UH ...

HEY, CONAN. DO YOU KNOW?

ORO? ORON-GUTAN?

WHAT KIND OF LOGIC IS THAT?

IT'S SHORT FOR "OH, WHAT A BIG RICH TREASURE!!"

IN OTHER WORDS...

THE FIRST "O" IS FOR "OH, HOW BIG!" "R" IS FOR "RICH!" AND THE LAST "O" IS FOR "OH, WHAT A TREASURE!"

←ORO

OH, PLEASE...

AW... WELL, YEAH!

WOW, MITCH!! YOU'RE SUPER SMART!!

I'LL BUY A SPACE SHUTTLE FROM NASA AND FLY TO OUTER SPACE.

I'M GONNA TRAVEL AROUND THE WORLD A HUNDRED TIMES!

I'M GONNA USE THAT TREASURE TO EAT ALL THE GRILLED EELS IN THE WORLD!!

IT MUST BE AN AWESOME TREASURE.

HELLO!

DREAM DREAM DREAM

SORRY...

HOW BORING...

UH... I'LL SAVE IT.

AND YOU, CONAN?

TOTO TOWER...

ALL RIGHT, THIS IS WHERE WE START!!

HMM...

!?

I CAN'T TELL WHAT'S WHAT! THE OTHER DRAWINGS ARE ALL SUCH FUNNY SHAPES.

NOW ALL WE HAVE TO DO IS CRACK THE CODE.

BUT...

IT'S THE MOON!! THE MOON!!

OH, I GOT IT!

.....

THEN DO *YOU* KNOW WHERE IT IS !?

BESIDES, YOU WOULDN'T BE ABLE TO PINPOINT AN ACCURATE LOCATION WITH A DRAWING THIS SIMPLE.

THE MOON CHANGES POSITION DEPENDING ON THE DAY.

I BET FROM THE SPOT THE TREASURE IS HIDDEN, THE MOON APPEARS NEXT TO THE TOWER LIKE THIS.

HA HA HA. THAT'S UNLIKELY.

FOR EXAMPLE, THE DIAGRAM BELOW THE TOWER COULD BE A HAT, THE ONE BELOW IT UNDERPANTS, AND BELOW THAT A BOW TIE.

THE THING THAT TIES THEM TOGETHER MIGHT BE--

Y-YEAH ...I'M LOOKING AT THE OTHER DIAGRAMS.

I THINK THEY COULD BE SIMPLIFIED SHAPES OF THINGS.

DID YOU FIGURE SOMETHING OUT, CONAN?

A CLOTHING STORE!!!

OH!

GUYS!!

DASH

W-WAIT!

HUH?

BUT THAT'S NOT ENOUGH TO--

Terahara Clothing Store

FAT CHANCE ...

ITALIAN !?

!?

IT MUST BE AN ACRONYM OR AN ABBREVIATION.

NO ... IT'S NOT IN HERE.

BUT NOW I HAVE NO IDEA ...

!?

IT'S ITALIAN FOR GOLD !!!

ornitorinco （名·男）[ ]
órno （名·男）［植］=orenel
òro （名·男）①金(Au), 黄金.
~ nero 石炭, 石油.
②金貨, 金銭, 富.

TH-THERE IT IS! ORO MEANS GOLD!!

IT MIGHT REALLY LEAD TO TREASURE !

←ORO

WAIT A SEC. THEN THIS CODE ...

... AND THE LOCATION OF THE 15,000 MAPLE LEAF GOLD COINS THEY STOLE IS STILL UNKNOWN.

HIS PARTNERS ARE STILL AT LARGE IN JAPAN ...

HE WILL BE EXTRADITED TO ITALY TOMORROW MORNING.

THE RINGLEADER OF THE ITALIAN GANG OF BURGLARS, DINO CAPANE, WAS APPREHENDED RECENTLY HERE IN JAPAN ....

HEY, LOOK AT THIS MESS.

HMM... ¥600 MILLION? WHAT BOLD GUYS.

PWIIK

ADJUSTED INTO YEN, THESE COINS ARE WORTH AROUND ¥600 MILLION. THEY WERE STOLEN FROM ITALY'S PASTA BANK ONE YEAR AGO.

RICHARD MOORE P.I.

JEEZ ... KIDS ARE SO CAREFREE.

GLUG

IF YOU'RE TALKING ABOUT CONAN, HE WENT OUT TO PLAY EARLY THIS MORNING!

WHERE'S THE LITTLE TWIRP?

HUH?

YOU'RE SUCH A SLOB!

ONE OF THE PARTNERS HAS BEEN IDENTIFIED AS BEING JAPANESE.

ACCORDING TO ITALIAN POLICE, CAPANE HAS THREE PARTNERS.

FINE, FINE ...

C'MON DAD! HELP ME CLEAN A LITTLE!

IS IT A MAP? OR SOME KIND OF MESSAGE?

WHAT IS THIS CODE ?

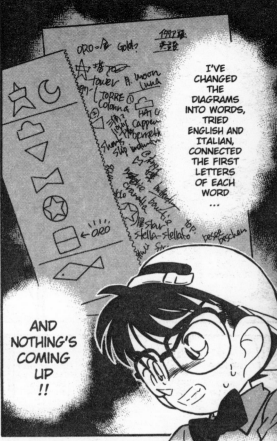

I'VE CHANGED THE DIAGRAMS INTO WORDS, TRIED ENGLISH AND ITALIAN, CONNECTED THE FIRST LETTERS OF EACH WORD ...

.....

AGH! DARN IT!!

AND NOTHING'S COMING UP !!

HUH ?

MAYBE *THAT'S* IT!

HEY, LOOK! LOOK!

HEY ...

YOU'RE RIGHT.

IT'S EXACTLY LIKE THE SECOND DRAWING!

SIGN!?

SEE THAT SIGN!?

CAFE TERRACE

julei.

MAYBE THESE DRAWINGS...

THEN MAYBE...

BUT THE ROAD SPLITS INTO TWO UP AHEAD.

THEN IF WE FOLLOW THE SIGNS SHAPED LIKE THESE DRAWINGS, WE'LL FIND THE TREASURE!

I BET THIS CODE IS MADE UP OF THE SHAPES OF SIGNS!

THAT *HAS* TO BE IT! THE SHOP IS RIGHT IN FRONT OF TOTO TOWER.

I THINK THIS STREET...

WAIT A SEC...

WHICH STREET!?

UNLESS WE KNOW WHICH STREET TO TAKE, IT'S HOPELESS.

ROAD MAP

CAN IT BE THAT THE MOON NEXT TO THE TOWER INDICATES TSUKIMI STREET?

IT'S CALLED TSUKIMI STREET-- MOONVIEW STREET!!

Toto Tower

Tsukimi Street

LET'S GO CHECK IT OUT!

ROAD MAP

HEY !!

TMP TMP TMP

DASH

TSUKIMI STREET IS ON THE RIGHT ...

SO THEN THIS DIAGRAM REALLY IS...

YOU'RE RIGHT! IT'S EXACTLY LIKE THE THIRD DRAWING !!

Family Restaurant

DONNL'S

THERE IT IS! AN UPSIDE-DOWN TRIANGLE !!!

!?

THAT'S IT... I GOT IT!!

AN AQUARIUM!?

HUH?

3 km ahead
Nambu Aquarium

AND...

AND...

DASH

WHAT LIES AHEAD IS...

IN OTHER WORDS, IT INDICATES THE SIGNS ALONG TSUKIMI STREET!!

THIS CODE IS A MAP FROM TOTO TOWER TO NAMBU AQUARIUM!!

←ORO

FILE 9:
THE ANSWER AND
ANOTHER ANSWER

LOOK!

DA DA DA....

A SIGN SHAPED LIKE A BOW TIE !!

Kishida Pharmacy

THERE IT IS !

THE MOON NEXT TO IT REPRESENTS TSUKIMI STREET.

THE FIRST DIAGRAM IS TOTO TOWER.

AND THE LAST DIAGRAM REPRESENTS NAMBU AQUARIUM.

←ORO

SEE! IT'S EXACTLY LIKE THE FOURTH DRAWING !!

←ORO

THIS CONFIRMS IT.

IT SHOWS THE SIGNS ALONG TSUKIMI STREET-- WHICH IS THE STREET CONNECTING TOTO TOWER AND THE NAMBU AQUARIUM!!

IN OTHER WORDS, THIS CODE ...

THERE'S NO MISTAKE!

YAY

ALL RIGHT. TWO MORE SIGNS TO GO!!

AND THE ORO WRITTEN NEXT TO THE SIXTH DIAGRAM MEANS "GOLD" IN ITALIAN.

THIS CODE INDICATES THE LOCATION OF GOLD.

DASH

IT'S A REAL TREASURE MAP!!

DARN IT! WE MUST BE SO CLOSE TO THE TREASURE.

WHERE'S THE FIFTH STAR-SHAPED SIGN?

HUF
HUF
HUF

HUF

PAPICO

HUF

HUF

WHAT!?

HEY, WE'RE ALREADY AT THE AQUARIUM.

Nambu Aquarium

THE FIFTH SIGN MUST HAVE BEEN BETWEEN THE TWO SOMEWHERE.

TSUKIMI STREET IS THE STREET FROM TOTO TOWER TO THE NAMBU AQUARIUM.

Tsukini Street

Yamakoshi Road

Nambu Aquarium

WH-WHAT'S GOING ON?

.....

SHFF

BINK

OR IS MY THEORY WRONG!?

IT'S THE GUY WE MET AT TOTO TOWER YESTERDAY. HE'S THE ONE WHO OWNS THIS CODE.

WHAT'S HE DOING HERE?

HEY, IT'S THAT GUY!

CAPANE'S PARTNERS IN THE ITALIAN GANG HAVE BEEN IDENTIFIED AS BEING THREE MEN. THEY ARE ON THE RUN.

HE'S WITH FOREIGNERS ...?

!?

THEIR WHEREABOUTS AND THAT OF THE 15,000 MAPLE LEAF GOLD COINS THEY STOLE IN ITALY ONE YEAR AGO ARE STILL UNKNOWN.

IT COULDN'T BE !?

NO ...

THREE MEN !?

FURTHER-MORE, THESE THREE MEN ...

GOLD COINS ?

ITALY ?

ARE THEY THE ITALIAN BURGLARS ON THE RUN!?

THOSE GUYS ...

IF THE PERSON WHO WROTE THIS WAS ITALIAN ...

THIS MOON ...

... WAIT A SECOND ...

ORO

IF THEY ARE ...

IT MAKES SENSE THAT "ORO" IS ITALIAN.

!?

JUST MAYBE ...

MAYBE ...

!!

LOOK AT THAT, RIGHT THERE!

.....

THE TREASURE'S IN THE GARBAGE!

WHO CARES!!

KAPPA

BUT WE HAVE NOT YET FOUND THE FIFTH STAR DRAWING.

WE PROBABLY JUST MISSED IT ...

HEY, IT'S EXACTLY LIKE THE SIXTH DRAWING!!

Ahead

Trash Collection Site

NOW THERE'S NO DANGER.

ALL RIGHT!

Trash Collection Site

BUT I CAN'T BELIEVE THAT CODE REALLY WAS A TREASURE MAP.

SHFF

AND THE BURGLARS GOT THE CODE BACK SO THEY WON'T BE FOLLOWING US ANYMORE.

AMY AND THE OTHERS ARE SAFE AND ON THEIR WAY HOME.

WELL THEN, I BETTER GET STARTED.

TUG

GOOD THING I PHOTOCOPIED IT AT THE BOOKSTORE.

HEH HEH HEH...

POINK

THE BOSS HID THE GOLD, AND NOW HIS PARTNERS ARE TRYING TO FIND IT USING THIS CODE.

JUDGING FROM THEIR CONVERSATION...

FWIP

ON WITH THE TREASURE HUNT !!!

THAT ☾ DIAGRAM ...

IT ACTUALLY INDICATES THE MOON ITSELF !!

THE PERSON WHO WROTE "ORO" IN ITALIAN ...

... WOULD BE UNLIKELY TO USE ☾ TO INDICATE TSUKIMI STREET-- A STREET NAMED IN JAPANESE.

MAN ...

WHAT A DUMB MISTAKE I MADE.

DASH

THINGS SUCH AS ...

FSHAA

SOME THINGS ARE ONLY VISIBLE AT NIGHT.

AND THE MOON INDICATES NIGHTTIME !

IN OTHER WORDS, I SHOULD LOOK FOR NEON SIGNS SHAPED LIKE THESE DRAWINGS, STARTING WITH THE TOP ONE.

← OREO

THAT'S RIGHT. THIS CODE IS A TREASURE MAP LISTING THE SHAPES OF NEON SIGNS.

NEON SIGNS !!

FROM EACH SIGN, I'LL GO TO THE NEXT ONE THAT CAN BE SEEN FROM THERE.

THAT SHOULD LEAD ME TO WHERE THE GOLD COINS ARE HIDDEN.

LOOKS LIKE I'M RIGHT THIS TIME.

WE'RE NOT GONNA LET YOU GET AWAY WITH THIS!!

... AND GO TO THE POLICE.

ALL RIGHT, I'LL FIND THE GOLD COINS BEFORE THE BURGLARS ...

HUH?

FSHAA

G-GUYS ...

GLARE

HOW DO WE GET TO THE TREASURE!?

NOW TELL US, CONAN!!

UM, UH ...

YEAH, CONAN!!

HEH HEH. YOU CAN'T FOOL THESE EYES OF MINE.

YOU WERE GONNA STEAL THE TREASURE FOR YOURSELF, WEREN'T YOU!?

NO FAIR, CONAN!!

I-I CAN EXPLAIN ...

OH, IT'S A PIECE OF CAKE.

BUT IT LOOKS LIKE THE GANG IS NOT AFTER US ANYMORE, SO...

GLANCE

I GUESS IT'S OKAY.

WE JUST HAVE TO FOLLOW THE NEON SIGNS, HUH?

Butweiser

DARN IT! I SENT YOU GUYS HOME FOR YOUR OWN SAFETY.

CHILD'S PLAY, REALLY.

BEATS ME!

WHERE IS IT, CONAN!?

THAT'S STRANGE. ONCE AGAIN, THE FIFTH STAR-SHAPED ONE IS NOWHERE TO BE FOUND.

HUH?

COME OVER HERE, GUYS!!

DASH

A FERRIS WHEEL!!

I BET THAT'S IT!!!

THEN THE SIXTH ONE SHOULDN'T BE TOO FAR EITHER.

IT WAS RIGHT IN FRONT OF US.

MUST BE SO. IT MATCHES THE FIFTH DRAWING.

THE SIXTH NEON SIGN!!

銘酒

鬼桜

THERE IT IS!!

HEY!

HEY, CONAN. THE TREASURE BETTER REALLY BE HERE.

IT SAYS "ORO" NEXT TO THIS SIXTH DRAWING!

... IS THAT LAST FISH-SHAPED THING THAT WE'RE SUPPOSED TO BE ABLE TO SEE FROM HERE.

BUT WHAT I CAN'T SEEM TO FIND ...

I DON'T SEE ANY NEON SIGN SHAPED LIKE A FISH, EITHER.

NATURALLY. THIS IS AN ORDINARY RESIDENTIAL AREA. THERE'S NOT EVEN A FISH STORE, LET ALONE AN AQUARIUM.

HEY ...

ALL RIGHT, LET'S CHECK OUT THE RIVER!!

DASH

THAT'S IT! IT MUST MEAN FISH IN THE RIVER!!

HUH ?

RIVER ?

I MEAN, THERE'S A RIVER NEARBY BUT--

156

HEY, GEORGE, LET'S GO HOME.

NO. THAT CODE IS A MAP OF THINGS THAT CAN ONLY BE SEEN AT NIGHT.

IT DOESN'T MAKE SENSE FOR THE LAST DRAWING OF THE FISH TO REPRESENT THE RIVER.

WAH! PLONK

SHUT UP! THE TREASURE'S GOTTA BE AT THE BOTTOM OF THIS RIVER!!

IT'S DANGEROUS.

SPLASH

THERE MUST BE A FISH-SHAPED NEON SIGN!!!

IF MY THEORY IS CORRECT, IT MUST BE SOMEWHERE CLOSE BY!!

FILE·10: THE GLOWING FISH

YEAH...

THE GLOWING FISH?

I FOUND THE GLOWING FISH.

←OR

BUT... I JUST FOUND IT.

WE GOT HERE BY FOLLOWING THOSE SHAPES, BUT WE JUST COULDN'T FIND THE FISH SHAPE HERE AT THE BOTTOM.

THIS CODE IS MADE OF SHAPES MADE BY NEON SIGNS OR LIGHTS, AND THEY CAN ONLY BE SEEN AT NIGHT.

←ORO

I'M SAYING I FOUND NEON LIGHTS IN THE SHAPE OF A FISH!

I DON'T SEE ANY GLOWING FISH SWIMMING ANWHERE!!

WHERE? WHERE?

SPLASH

HEY, WAIT!

JUST FOLLOW ME!

DASH

WHAT WOULD A GLOWING FISH BE DOING UP HERE!?

C'MON, HURRY!

CREAK

CLANK CLANK CLANK

MAN ...

JUST LOOK OUTSIDE FROM HERE!

IT'S PITCH DARK. I CAN'T SEE ANY-THING, LET ALONE A FISH!!

THERE IT IS.

SEE? OVER THERE ...

TOWARD THE RIVER ...

RIVER ?

THERE'S THE GLOWING FISH!!

... CAME TO THIS BUILDING WITH THE SIXTH NEON SIGN, THEN CLIMBED UP HERE.

IN OTHER WORDS, THE PERSON WHO WROTE THIS CODE ...

←ORO

AND THE LIGHT ON TOP OF THE BUILDING ACROSS THE WAY BECOMES THE EYE!!

WITH THE REFLECTION IN THE WATER, THE LIGHTS ON THE BRIDGE FORM A FISH SHAPE!

HOW'RE WE GONNA FIND IT, CONAN?

I DON'T SEE ANY LIGHTS, EITHER.

BUT... IT'S PITCH DARK!

THEN THE TREASURE'S SOME-WHERE UP HERE!?

AND FROM HERE YOU CAN SEE THE BRIDGE CLEARLY BECAUSE THE OTHER BUILDINGS DON'T OBSTRUCT THE VIEW!

WH-WHERE?

CALM DOWN. THIS CODE SHOWS THE LOCATION OF THE TREASURE!

... LOOKS EXACTLY LIKE THIS DRAWING.

I BET THERE'S ONLY ONE SPOT HERE WHERE THE BRIDGE...

SEE THIS FISH SHAPE!?

HERE!

......

SCOOT

THE TREASURE IS PROBABLY THERE.

IT'S RIGHT HERE!!

←oeo

YEAH...

6

A GOLD COIN.

MM?

CLINK

THE BAG OF GOLD COINS IS TIED TO A ROPE AND HANGING FROM THE BEAM.

AND THE ROPES ARE HOOKED OVER THERE.

THAT'S IT!

LOOKS LIKE IT'S ATTACHED TO A ROPE.

WHAT'S THAT BLACK SHADOW!?

!?

WBBL

YANK

ALL RIGHT, IF THAT'S THE CASE...

IT'S THE TREASURE!!

DASH

THE TREASURE!

WHOA!!

CLINK

HUH?

TUP

THE BURGLARS ON THE RUN!

GOOD JOB, KIDS.

!?

GIVE IT BACK! WE FOUND THAT TREASURE!!

GEORGE...

BONK WHAK SMAK

WHO ARE THOSE MEN?

SO... THEY HAVEN'T FIGURED OUT WHERE THEY'RE STASHED.

ARE THEY LOOKING FOR THE COINS?

ARE YOU OKAY, GEORGE?

RATS!

AND NO ONE KNOWS WHERE THE STOLEN GOLD COINS ARE HIDDEN.

I SAW IT ON TV. THE LEADER OF AN ITALIAN GANG OF BURGLARS, A GUY NAMED CAPANE, WAS ARRESTED IN JAPAN TWO DAYS AGO. HIS THREE PARTNERS ARE STILL ON THE RUN.

A G-GANG OF BURGLARS?

AN ITALIAN GANG OF BURGLARS!

EXACTLY, MY BOY.

... THESE GOLD COINS ARE ...

ARE YOU SAYING ...

HE TOOK THE 15,000 STOLEN MAPLE LEAF GOLD COINS WITH HIM.

BUT CAPANE BETRAYED US AND DISAPPEARED.

WE STOLE THE GOLD COINS FROM AN ITALIAN BANK ONE YEAR AGO ...

... UNDER ORDERS FROM OUR BOSS, CAPANE.

!?

WE SHOOK HIM DOWN BUT HE WOULDN'T TELL US ANYTHING.

ALL WE COULD FIND IN HIS ROOM WAS THIS CODE.

WE FOUND OUT SOME TIME LATER HE WAS IN JAPAN, BUT BY THE TIME WE BUSTED INTO HIS HIDEOUT HE'D HIDDEN THE GOLD.

BUT YOU GUYS KEPT CRACKING THE CODE WHERE WE COULDN'T, SO WE LET YOU SWIM.

WE THOUGHT ABOUT TAKING IT FROM YOU GUYS BY FORCE...

SHFF

AT LEAST, WE WERE UNTIL YOU TOOK THE CODE FROM US.

GULP

...AND WE STARTED LOOKING FOR THE GOLD COINS USING THIS CODE.

THERE WASN'T MUCH WE COULD DO, SO WE TOLD THE COPS WHERE TO FIND HIM...

CHAK

'COURSE, WE NEVER THOUGHT YOU'D ACTUALLY FIND IT.

HURRY UP!!

NOW SPIT IT OUT!! WHERE'S THE GOLD!?

I KNOW YOU FOUND IT!

OR YOU'RE DEAD!!

I... I SEE...

YOU KNOW, THE FISH ON THE CODE. THE GOLD IS HIDDEN AT THE PLACE WHERE THE NIGHT VIEW OF THE BRIDGE MATCHES THAT FISH SHAPE.

THE FISH...

?

ONCE THEY FIND THE TREASURE, THEY'LL KILL US!

DUMMY! WHY'D YOU TELL HIM?

THEY'LL KILL US REGARDLESS!

THEY'LL TRAP US IN CEMENT AND SINK US IN THE OCEAN!

NO, THEY'LL BURN US TO DEATH SO THERE'S NO EVIDENCE...

OHH... WE'LL BE SHOT TO DEATH.

IT'S TOO EARLY TO GIVE UP!!

WAAAAH...

UNH...

DADDY...

MOM...

WE STILL HAVE A CHANCE.

HUH ?

WE ONLY HAVE ONE CHANCE.

STAND UP QUIETLY SO THEY DON'T NOTICE.

...THEY'LL BE DISTRACTED.

WHEN THEY FIND THE GOLD COINS...

WHFF

NOW !!

WE'LL SEIZE THAT MOMENT !!

REALLY ...?

HEH HEH ...

HE WAS SO COOL !!

IT WAS CONAN !!

CHU ♥

HUH ?

THANKS, CONAN. ♥

D-DON'T GET THE WRONG IDEA!

AW, YOU'RE EMBARRASSED. HOW CUTE!

RICHARD MOORE P.I.

WAIT, UH ...

THAT'S NOT HOW IT IS.

YOU JUST GOT YOURSELF A CUTE GIRLFRIEND.

OH! LUCKY YOU, CONAN!

THE ALCOHOLIC DETECTIVE YUTAKA TANI SERIES FILE 1995

A SUPPRESSED DESIRE TO KILL

AC Conan

I'll go buy it.

Okay.

Chocolate, preferably. I suddenly feel like eating cake.

Oh!

I'll go buy it.

Fine, fine.

With whip cream on top.

Now I wanna eat pudding.

Chomp Chomp

It's freezing out.

You serious?

A green tea popsicle.

Suddenly, I want an ice cream stick.

Ice cream is best in winter!!

Shlurp Shlrup

Go ... ahead and die.

Do you have any medicine?

How odd ...

I got a stomach-ache.

Ow ow ow!

Capture Gosho Aoyama, the Super Evil Criminal !!

Gosho Aoyama
Detectives:
Yutaka Tani   Masaki Negishi
Eiichi Yamagishi   Kōichi Kishida
Keiji Aso

Detective Yamachan's Puppet Show
We're All Friends

The Report from Gishimasa --
the ever-expanding Fat Detective
Is this what Aoyama Sensei is like?

What a pair of magical glasses! They let me talk to anything!

Hello, Yama-chan!

La La La

Hello!

All that's left is filling in the black and the screen-tones and my job is done.

Yay! I'm done with the pen.

Sensei's car!!

Let's talk to

Talk!!

Talk!

Please don't shake me.

Poor thing.

Hm, what? You're still working?

Mr. RX7?

It's fast, cool, and really expensive. The number one supercar in all of Japan, the RX7!

Wow!!

Call me when you're finished.

Yep.

Then I'll be playing Virtua Fighter!

The battery's dead.

It hasn't been driven for six months.

It's dead!!!

Ack!!

Poor thing...

R.I.P.

It's okay. It's mine.

Um, Aoyama Sensei? There's a blank sheet here.

What?

177

Keiji Aso: Head Detective
DON'T SAY BANZAI!

What!? I'm sorry but could you write another 4 panel strip for the end of the graphic novel.

Please...

Fine, I'll do it!

stare

...

Yay! I'm done!

No...

RIP RIP

This ain't going in MY book!

● THE END ●

~~BIG HEAD~~ YOUTHFUL STORYTELLER DETECTIVE
What is Youth?

Criminal!

You criminal!

Waa Waaa! Why?

You criminal!

Don't pick on criminals!

Stop!

"Fight," "Right," "Light and Might!"

Everybody! Recall those glorious, sparkling days and these words...

There There

Sniff Sniff

And... and... "Youth!" Oops.

Such beautiful words...

Aah, that takes me back...

Waaa

I messed up.

Did that rhyme?

Hello, Aoyama here.

Some folks claim that Dr. Watson's name should be rendered in Japanese as "wa-to-su-n." I've decided to go with "wa-to-so-n," the way it was written in the books that I read as a child. I wish the way names are written wouldn't change so much just for the sake of pronunciation. Even the name Poirot is being rendered now as "po-wa-ro" instead of "po-a-ro" as it has always been. But if they ever change the rendering of "Holmes" from "ho--mu-zu" to "ho-u-mu-zu" I think I'll cry.

ARSENE LUPIN

The gentleman thief Arsene Lupin—a man who can crack a smile even when he's about to face certain death!! Heavy-duty safes and security systems mean nothing to the protean Lupin. He's so masterful at the art of disguise that he sometimes even forgets what his own face looks like! He's so proficient at changing his voice and his handwriting that he'll never be caught! Arsene Lupin has even transformed himself into an officer of the law to solve a crime or two. And despite the difficult circumstances of his upbringing he still hasn't lost his sense of justice. Offering aid to the weak and defeating the strong, he has a particular weakness for a damsel in distress. To come to the aid of a fair maiden, he'll throw himself into all matter of danger. Arsene Lupin is indeed a daring grand master thief! By the way, have you readers figured out where Rachel Moore's original name Ran Mori came from? It's inspired from the name of the creator of Arsene Lupin, Maurice Leblanc. Rendered in Japanese it is "Mo—ri-su Ru-bu-ran." I recommend reading **The Extraordinary Adventures of Arsene Lupin, Gentleman Burglar.**

ALSO AVAILABLE FROM GOLLANCZ MANGA

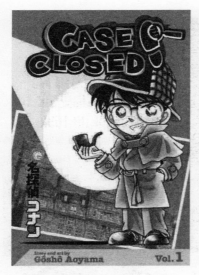

Precocious high school student Jimmy Kudo uses his keen powers of observation and astute intuition to solve mysteries that have left police baffled. Hot on the trail of a suspect, Jimmy is accosted from behind and fed a strange chemical which physically transforms him into a grade schooler!

Taking on the pseudonym Conan Edogawa, he attempts to track down who did this to him. But until he finds a cure for his bizarre condition, Jimmy continues to help the police solve their toughest cases.

find out more at www.orionbooks.co.uk

ALSO AVAILABLE FROM GOLLANCZ MANGA

Miaka Yûki is an ordinary junior high student who is suddenly transported into the world of a book, THE UNIVERSE OF THE FOUR GODS.

Surrounded by enemies with mystic power, she can only rely on her Celestial Warriors and a mysterious monk, a disciple of the oracle, to help her fulfill her quest!

find out more at www.orionbooks.co.uk

OUT NOW FROM GOLLANCZ MANGA

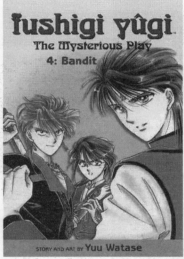

fushigi yûgi
The Mysterious Play
4: Bandit

STORY AND ART BY **Yuu Watase**

Miaka Yûki is an ordinary junior-high-school student who is transported into the world of a book, THE UNIVERSE OF THE FOUR GODS.

She encounters base villains and dashing heroes, and still manages to worry about her grades and where her next banquet is coming from.

Miaka must find the three remaining Celestial Warriors — but her search leads her to a bandit-lair and a plague-cursed town where she has to die to survive!

GOLLANCZ MANGA

find out more at www.orionbooks.co.uk

COMING SOON FROM GOLLANCZ MANGA

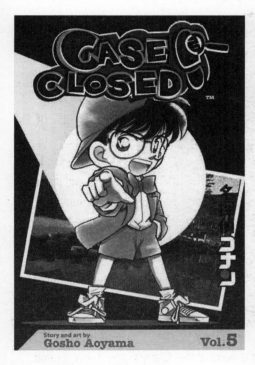

Precocious high school student Jimmy Kudo uses his keen powers of observation and astute intuition to solve mysteries that have left police baffled. Hot on the trail of a suspect, Jimmy is accosted from behind and fed a strange chemical which physically transforms him into a grade schooler!

Bloody murders, treasure hunts and the return of the sinister men in black — watch out for the all-new adventures of Jimmy Kudo in Case Closed!

find out more at www.orionbooks.co.uk

COMING SOON FROM GOLLANCZ MANGA

fushigi yûgi
The Mysterious Play
Vol. 5: RIVAL

STORY AND ART BY **Yuu Watase**

Miaka Yûki is an ordinary junior-high student who is transported into the world of a book, THE UNIVERSE OF THE FOUR GODS.

She encounters base villains and dashing heroes, and still managed to worry about her grades and where her next banquet is coming from. To save her newly adopted country of Hong-Nan, Miaka must venture into the heart of the enemy's capital. Her mission: to retrieve her true love, Tamahome; outwit the unscrupulous General Nakaga; and confront Yui, the girl who was once her best friend, but is now her most vindictive rival!

GOLLANCZ MANGA

find out more at www.orionbooks.co.uk

COMING SOON FROM GOLLANCZ MANGA

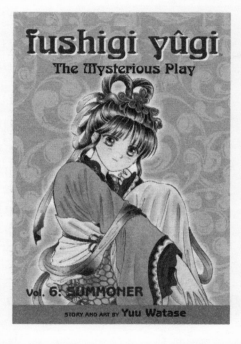

find out more at www.orionbooks.co.uk

COMING SOON FROM GOLLANCZ MANGA

It's Conan versus the Phantom Thief! Who is this mysterious masked man — and how does he know Conan's true identity? Find out, in the latest adventures of Jimmy Kudo in Case Closed!

find out more at www.orionbooks.co.uk